LOSING AND KEEPING OFF WEIGHT:
A WORKBOOK APPLYING JAMES CLEAR'S
ATOMIC HABITS

BY JAMES HENRY

Preface

If you've read James Clear's *Atomic Habits*, then you've already read the basic principles needed to lose and keep off excess fat because the secret to successful weight loss is found in habits, small habits that make a big difference. However, you need to apply Clear's principles! That is where this book comes in. With it, you'll find yourself successfully forming habits that leave you fitter and healthier.

Maybe you've read my previous workbook that takes the effort out of forming habits. This book is based on that book and gives templates and advice customized for losing weight and keeping it off.

Over the last century, perhaps because delicious food has become ever more accessible and prevalent and perhaps for more complicated reasons, the world has been gaining weight. Surely you've noticed it, and as a reader of this book you've probably noticed excess fat on yourself. Do know: *this is nothing to be ashamed about!* This is a global issue that no individual can take blame for, particularly *you*. That said, each of us as individuals can take our health into our own hands and through atomic habits can change ourselves into a fitter, leaner, healthier version of ourselves.

Let me know how this workbook is working for you. You can reach me at jimrobhenry@gmail.com.

Regards,
James Henry

Outline and Guide to the Journal:

Identity (Pages 1-4)

Behavior is ruled by identity and the key to changing behavior is to change identity. Our identity changes when there is a change of habit. Weight, fitness, health, these are wrapped up in our identities. In this section you will outline your desired identity. This section has 3 main prompts that guide you.
- Brainstorm
- Organize
- Formalize

Habits to Make or Break (Pages 5-8)

In this section you will list your current habits and will analyze them determining what is promoting your desired identity and what is not. You'll also decide on new habits you want to incorporate into your life and make plans on how to apply the 4 laws of habits.
- Habits Scorecard
- New Habits List
- New Habits to Make
- Habits to Break

Habit Tracker (Pages 9-10)

This section offers a way to track your habits easily.

Review and Reflect (Pages 11-12)

As you progress, you'll need to take time to review your habits and reflect on your identity. Are you going in the right direction or are some of your habits not quite right? This section gives some prompts to discover what's up.

Templates (Pages 13-119)

In this section you'll find
- 25 habit making templates on pages 14-63,
- 25 habit breaking templates are on pages 64-113, and
- 6 extra habit trackers are found on pages 114-119.

Of course, if you find that you have more success doing things a bit differently than outlined, then do that! I hope that this journal allows for flexibility and caters to many different people's needs.

Identity

What Is Your Desired Identity?

Your identity shapes your behaviors and motivations, and habits shape your identity. Each habit acts as evidence of what sort of a person you are.

When overweight, the desire to lose weight in a healthy way is a desire to change your identity for the better. To change your identity, you'll need to change your habits and your desired identity informs what habits need what changes. The next several pages help you discover and articulate this desired identity.

Before you start, note that there are a number of identities that are related to weight loss and maintenance of a healthy weight.

- There are those that take a new diet on as part of their identity. Similar to how some avoid alcohol or pork because of their religious identity, you reinforce compliance to a diet avoiding processed foods, added sugars, or refined carbohydrates by making it part of who you are, part of your identity.
- Some people identify themselves as meticulous, scientific, or data driven. They'll use this identity to succeed in careful calorie tracking, weight tracking, and perhaps even modeling their metabolism.
- Others lose weight by identifying as an epicurean. They decide to become very discerning about and interested in taste. In order to eat most deliciously, they will stop eating once one bite is less exhilarating than the bite before it.
- And still others may go the ascetic route. Through intermittently fasting, eating only potatoes for two out of their three meals, or many other practices they support their identity and lose weight.
- Also, don't forget the social aspects of your identity. Eating, and thus weight management, is often a very social activity. Joining a health-related group or getting friends and family to join or create your own group that reinforces health can be a strong part of your identity.

I would advise not letting fear into your identity. Calorie counting, avoiding certain foods, eating more fiber, failing and having to try again, etc.—these things needn't be scary, and by cultivating a new identity through new habits, you can lose whatever fears and insecurities you may have around losing weight.

Now, to make your desired identity concrete, you'll want to brainstorm ideas, organize them, and then finalize them into a clear statement, perhaps one that is worth memorizing or at least frequently reviewing.

Writing out your desired identity like this is helpful in several ways. First, it helps you realize what goals you need to be setting. Since identity leads to outcomes, you'll want to set habits that support your desired identity. Second, having a written, formal statement of who you want to be helps to motivate you, it makes your goals more attractive and accomplishing them more satisfying.

Brainstorm

What is your desired identity? Use the following lines to brainstorm ideas.

You may want to brainstorm *outcomes* you want (a goal weight or a waist size).

Then consider what is the *process* that would lead to this outcome. This could include things like eating less, eating healthier, or exercising more. As this is a place for brainstorming, feel free to get as specific or general as is helpful.

Finally, what sort of an *identity* supports the processes that lead to the desired outcomes. Note that identities, since they are made up of habits, can include habits in their descriptions. Some examples of attributes of an identity include "health conscious," "active," "mindful eater," "health guru," "athlete," etc. Others may include relationships like "mother" or "father" as such an identity may motivate weight loss in order to help you envision enjoying time with children and future grandchildren.

_____

_____

_____

_____

_____

_____

_____

_____

_____

_____

_____

_____

_____

_____

_____

_____

_____

_____

_____

_____

Organize and Formalize

Organize and formalize the ideas that you brainstormed into a cohesive written statement. This may be something that you memorize or that you review to internalize your identity and to remember why you are working on specific habits.

Your written statement could look like this, "My Desired Identity: I am a big hiker which requires me to be physically fit. I'm a healthy eater who eats lots of fibrous, high satiety foods. I am someone who follows a schedule and thus I almost only ever eat at set meal times."

_____

_____

_____

_____

_____

_____

_____

_____

_____

_____

_____

_____

_____

_____

_____

_____

_____

_____

_____

_____

_____

_____

_____

Habits to Make or Break

Now you will make the plans to change your current identity to your desired identity. As James Clear points out, the key to attaining your desired identity is to change your habits.

Habit Scorecard

In James Clear's book, he talks about writing out a habit scorecard. This scorecard is a list of all the habits that you have right now, this may include eating breakfast, brushing teeth, etc. After listing your habits out, you put a "+" next to those habits that are in line with your desired identity and a "-" next to those that go against your desired identity. In this way you get a sense of what habits you should continue and which you should break. Note that some habits may not have a "+" or "-" next to them.

You'll want to do this even for habits that aren't directly related to your identity because knowing all your habits can help you to form new ones by linking new habits with old habits.

Right here, use the lines to list out your habits and then to score them "+" or "-".

_____

_____

_____

_____

_____

_____

_____

_____

_____

_____

_____

_____

New Habits List

Now, list what new habits you want to incorporate into your life. Of course, these new habits should be supporting your desired identity.

Note that this isn't a list of only the habits you'll be working on immediately. Some of these habits you'll work on first and others you may incorporate later. Improvement and change don't happen all at once.

_____

_____

_____

_____

_____

_____

_____

_____

_____

_____

_____

_____

_____

_____

_____

_____

_____

_____

_____

_____

_____

_____

_____

_____

_____

_____

Looking at your list of new desired habits and at those habits that got a "-" score on the scorecard, circle or highlight a few habits that you think are best to work on now. Your desired identity and your circumstances will be helpful to guide you to know which habits and how many habits to first focus on and which may be better to incorporate into your life later.

New Habits to Make

For each of the new habits you want to work on, consider the following questions that follow James Clear's "Four Laws of Habits." Write your answers in one of the "New Habit to Make" templates that start on page 14.

Law 1
- What is the habit you want to make?
- When and where will it be done? (Maybe use one of Clear's patterns: "I will [BEHAVIOR] at [TIME] in [Location]" or "After [CURRENT HABIT], I will [NEW HABIT]".)
- How can you set up your environment to make it easy and obvious to do?
- How else can you make obvious cues to prompt you to do the habit?

Law 2
- What's motivating you to do this habit?
- Is there some reward you will get or give yourself if you accomplish the habit? or maybe a rewarding activity right before the habit?
- Are there other people to help push you to do this habit?

Law 3
- How can you make it easier to do the habit?
- Can the environment or your schedule be set up so that the habit can be accomplished more easily?
- Can you automate or simplify your habit?
- Will Clear's "Two-minute Rule" help?

Law 4
- How will this habit be more satisfying?
- Will you reward yourself for completing it?
- Will you use a habit tracker for this habit? (see page 9)
- What will you do if you fail to do the habit once?

Habits to Break

For each of those habits you want to break, consider these questions, and write your answers in one of the "Habit to Break" templates that start on page 64.

Law 1
- What is the habit you want to break?
- When and where are cues that lead to this habit and how do you avoid these cues?
- How can you set up your environment to avoid cues?

Law 2
- What's motivating you to get rid of this habit?
- What benefits or rewards are there is you avoid this habit?
- Are there other people to help push you to avoid this habit?

Law 3
- How can you make it harder to do this habit?
- Can the environment or your schedule be set up so that the habit is difficult to do?

Law 4
- How can you make it less satisfying to do this habit?
- Is there someone you can ask to watch your behavior or to whom you can be accountable to?
- Will you use a habit tracker to track not doing this habit? (see page 9)
- What will you do if you fail to break the habit once?
- Can you set up a way to make the results of this bad habit public and painful?

Habit Tracker

There are a lot of different styles of habit tracker that may be used. Some may be more useful for certain habits than others. The next page has a habit tracker style that is flexible enough for most habits. Use it to make accomplishing your habits more satisfying. Also note that there are several more trackers in templates section on page 114 of this journal so that when this one is filled you can keep going.

Some people find it motivating to color code their habit tracking or organizing it in other visually pleasing ways. I personally find a simple checkmark is enough for me and it keeps it simple and easy.

Keeping track of metrics is helpful in any habit. Some especially useful metrics related to health and weight loss are first, of course, your weight, and then the circumference of your waist. This tracker is good for keeping track of these metrics as well as for tracking habits.

One thing to note about measurements though. There can be day to day fluctuation that can obscure longer term trends. If you are weighing yourself, be sure to consider this.

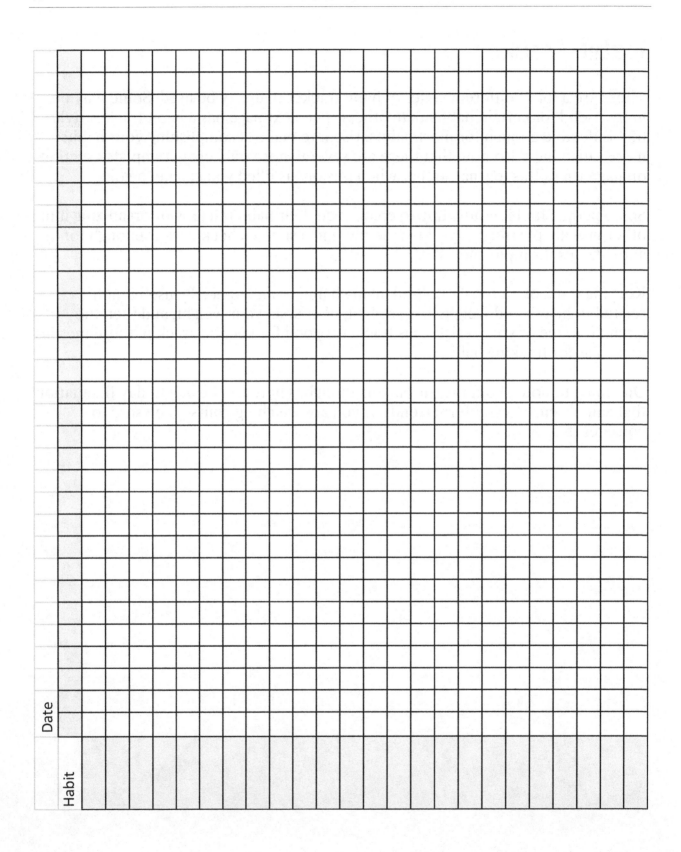

Review and Reflect

Review and reflection are important in order to continually foster habits and to continually become exponentially better. We need to know if our habits are working their desired change in us, and if they aren't we need to alter them.

Choose a periodic time and place where you will review how you are doing. By applying the 4 laws of habits, I've gotten in the habit of planning my next day out every evening. Every first Sunday of the month I take a little extra time to review and reflect on not just the last months habits, but also what I want from the future and how I will continue to progress.

Here are some questions that will help to ensure you are progressing.

What do you feel about your current habits (review and perhaps redo the habit scorecard)?

Has your desired identity changed? If so, update it and perhaps brainstorm, organize, and formalize your desired identity anew.

What new habits should you be incorporating?

Are there some habits that need to be broken?

Are some of the habits you've been working on needing extra attention?

Remember, tiny changes make a big difference. What tiny things might you need to be focusing on?

Templates

New Habit to Make

Law 1
- What is the habit you want to make?
- When and where will it be done? (Maybe use one of Clear's patterns: "I will [BEHAVIOR] at [TIME] in [Location]" or "After [CURRENT HABIT], I will [NEW HABIT]".)
- How can you set up your environment to make it easy and obvious to do?
- How else can you make obvious cues to prompt you to do the habit?

_____

_____

_____

_____

_____

Law 2
- What's motivating you to do this habit?
- Is there some reward you will get or give yourself if you accomplish the habit? or maybe a rewarding activity right before the habit?
- Are there other people to help push you to do this habit?

_____

_____

_____

_____

_____

Law 3
- How can you make it easier to do the habit?
- Can the environment or your schedule be set up so that the habit can be accomplished more easily?
- Can you automate or simplify your habit?
- Will Clear's "Two-minute Rule" help?

_____

_____

_____

_____

_____

Law 4
- How will this habit be more satisfying?
- Will you reward yourself for completing it?
- Will you use a habit tracker for this habit? (see page 9)
- What will you do if you fail to do the habit once?

_____

_____

_____

_____

_____

Any other notes for this habit?

_____

_____

_____

_____

_____

New Habit to Make

Law 1
- What is the habit you want to make?
- When and where will it be done? (Maybe use one of Clear's patterns: "I will [BEHAVIOR] at [TIME] in [Location]" or "After [CURRENT HABIT], I will [NEW HABIT]".)
- How can you set up your environment to make it easy and obvious to do?
- How else can you make obvious cues to prompt you to do the habit?

_____

_____

_____

_____

_____

Law 2
- What's motivating you to do this habit?
- Is there some reward you will get or give yourself if you accomplish the habit? or maybe a rewarding activity right before the habit?
- Are there other people to help push you to do this habit?

_____

_____

_____

_____

_____

Law 3
- How can you make it easier to do the habit?
- Can the environment or your schedule be set up so that the habit can be accomplished more easily?
- Can you automate or simplify your habit?
- Will Clear's "Two-minute Rule" help?

_____

_____

_____

_____

_____

Law 4

- How will this habit be more satisfying?
- Will you reward yourself for completing it?
- Will you use a habit tracker for this habit? (see page 9)
- What will you do if you fail to do the habit once?

_____

_____

_____

_____

_____

Any other notes for this habit?

_____

_____

_____

_____

_____

New Habit to Make

Law 1
- What is the habit you want to make?
- When and where will it be done? (Maybe use one of Clear's patterns: "I will [BEHAVIOR] at [TIME] in [Location]" or "After [CURRENT HABIT], I will [NEW HABIT]".)
- How can you set up your environment to make it easy and obvious to do?
- How else can you make obvious cues to prompt you to do the habit?

_____

_____

_____

_____

_____

Law 2
- What's motivating you to do this habit?
- Is there some reward you will get or give yourself if you accomplish the habit? or maybe a rewarding activity right before the habit?
- Are there other people to help push you to do this habit?

_____

_____

_____

_____

_____

Law 3
- How can you make it easier to do the habit?
- Can the environment or your schedule be set up so that the habit can be accomplished more easily?
- Can you automate or simplify your habit?
- Will Clear's "Two-minute Rule" help?

_____

_____

_____

_____

_____

Law 4
- How will this habit be more satisfying?
- Will you reward yourself for completing it?
- Will you use a habit tracker for this habit? (see page 9)
- What will you do if you fail to do the habit once?

_____

_____

_____

_____

_____

Any other notes for this habit?

_____

_____

_____

_____

_____

New Habit to Make

Law 1

- What is the habit you want to make?
- When and where will it be done? (Maybe use one of Clear's patterns: "I will [BEHAVIOR] at [TIME] in [Location]" or "After [CURRENT HABIT], I will [NEW HABIT]".)
- How can you set up your environment to make it easy and obvious to do?
- How else can you make obvious cues to prompt you to do the habit?

_____

_____

_____

_____

_____

Law 2

- What's motivating you to do this habit?
- Is there some reward you will get or give yourself if you accomplish the habit? or maybe a rewarding activity right before the habit?
- Are there other people to help push you to do this habit?

_____

_____

_____

_____

_____

Law 3

- How can you make it easier to do the habit?
- Can the environment or your schedule be set up so that the habit can be accomplished more easily?
- Can you automate or simplify your habit?
- Will Clear's "Two-minute Rule" help?

_____

_____

_____

_____

_____

Law 4

- How will this habit be more satisfying?
- Will you reward yourself for completing it?
- Will you use a habit tracker for this habit? (see page 9)
- What will you do if you fail to do the habit once?

_____

_____

_____

_____

_____

Any other notes for this habit?

_____

_____

_____

_____

_____

New Habit to Make

Law 1
- What is the habit you want to make?
- When and where will it be done? (Maybe use one of Clear's patterns: "I will [BEHAVIOR] at [TIME] in [Location]" or "After [CURRENT HABIT], I will [NEW HABIT]".)
- How can you set up your environment to make it easy and obvious to do?
- How else can you make obvious cues to prompt you to do the habit?

_____

_____

_____

_____

_____

Law 2
- What's motivating you to do this habit?
- Is there some reward you will get or give yourself if you accomplish the habit? or maybe a rewarding activity right before the habit?
- Are there other people to help push you to do this habit?

_____

_____

_____

_____

_____

Law 3
- How can you make it easier to do the habit?
- Can the environment or your schedule be set up so that the habit can be accomplished more easily?
- Can you automate or simplify your habit?
- Will Clear's "Two-minute Rule" help?

_____

_____

_____

_____

_____

Law 4

- How will this habit be more satisfying?
- Will you reward yourself for completing it?
- Will you use a habit tracker for this habit? (see page 9)
- What will you do if you fail to do the habit once?

_____

_____

_____

_____

_____

Any other notes for this habit?

_____

_____

_____

_____

_____

New Habit to Make

Law 1
- What is the habit you want to make?
- When and where will it be done? (Maybe use one of Clear's patterns: "I will [BEHAVIOR] at [TIME] in [Location]" or "After [CURRENT HABIT], I will [NEW HABIT]".)
- How can you set up your environment to make it easy and obvious to do?
- How else can you make obvious cues to prompt you to do the habit?

_____

_____

_____

_____

_____

Law 2
- What's motivating you to do this habit?
- Is there some reward you will get or give yourself if you accomplish the habit? or maybe a rewarding activity right before the habit?
- Are there other people to help push you to do this habit?

_____

_____

_____

_____

_____

Law 3
- How can you make it easier to do the habit?
- Can the environment or your schedule be set up so that the habit can be accomplished more easily?
- Can you automate or simplify your habit?
- Will Clear's "Two-minute Rule" help?

_____

_____

_____

_____

_____

Law 4

- How will this habit be more satisfying?
- Will you reward yourself for completing it?
- Will you use a habit tracker for this habit? (see page 9)
- What will you do if you fail to do the habit once?

_____

_____

_____

_____

_____

Any other notes for this habit?

_____

_____

_____

_____

_____

New Habit to Make

Law 1
- What is the habit you want to make?
- When and where will it be done? (Maybe use one of Clear's patterns: "I will [BEHAVIOR] at [TIME] in [Location]" or "After [CURRENT HABIT], I will [NEW HABIT]".)
- How can you set up your environment to make it easy and obvious to do?
- How else can you make obvious cues to prompt you to do the habit?

_____

_____

_____

_____

_____

Law 2
- What's motivating you to do this habit?
- Is there some reward you will get or give yourself if you accomplish the habit? or maybe a rewarding activity right before the habit?
- Are there other people to help push you to do this habit?

_____

_____

_____

_____

_____

Law 3
- How can you make it easier to do the habit?
- Can the environment or your schedule be set up so that the habit can be accomplished more easily?
- Can you automate or simplify your habit?
- Will Clear's "Two-minute Rule" help?

_____

_____

_____

_____

_____

Law 4

- How will this habit be more satisfying?
- Will you reward yourself for completing it?
- Will you use a habit tracker for this habit? (see page 9)
- What will you do if you fail to do the habit once?

_____

_____

_____

_____

_____

Any other notes for this habit?

_____

_____

_____

_____

_____

New Habit to Make

Law 1
- What is the habit you want to make?
- When and where will it be done? (Maybe use one of Clear's patterns: "I will [BEHAVIOR] at [TIME] in [Location]" or "After [CURRENT HABIT], I will [NEW HABIT]".)
- How can you set up your environment to make it easy and obvious to do?
- How else can you make obvious cues to prompt you to do the habit?

_____

_____

_____

_____

_____

Law 2
- What's motivating you to do this habit?
- Is there some reward you will get or give yourself if you accomplish the habit? or maybe a rewarding activity right before the habit?
- Are there other people to help push you to do this habit?

_____

_____

_____

_____

Law 3
- How can you make it easier to do the habit?
- Can the environment or your schedule be set up so that the habit can be accomplished more easily?
- Can you automate or simplify your habit?
- Will Clear's "Two-minute Rule" help?

_____

_____

_____

_____

Law 4

- How will this habit be more satisfying?
- Will you reward yourself for completing it?
- Will you use a habit tracker for this habit? (see page 9)
- What will you do if you fail to do the habit once?

_____

_____

_____

_____

_____

Any other notes for this habit?

_____

_____

_____

_____

_____

New Habit to Make

Law 1
- What is the habit you want to make?
- When and where will it be done? (Maybe use one of Clear's patterns: "I will [BEHAVIOR] at [TIME] in [Location]" or "After [CURRENT HABIT], I will [NEW HABIT]".)
- How can you set up your environment to make it easy and obvious to do?
- How else can you make obvious cues to prompt you to do the habit?

_____

_____

_____

_____

_____

Law 2
- What's motivating you to do this habit?
- Is there some reward you will get or give yourself if you accomplish the habit? or maybe a rewarding activity right before the habit?
- Are there other people to help push you to do this habit?

_____

_____

_____

_____

Law 3
- How can you make it easier to do the habit?
- Can the environment or your schedule be set up so that the habit can be accomplished more easily?
- Can you automate or simplify your habit?
- Will Clear's "Two-minute Rule" help?

_____

_____

_____

_____

_____

Law 4

- How will this habit be more satisfying?
- Will you reward yourself for completing it?
- Will you use a habit tracker for this habit? (see page 9)
- What will you do if you fail to do the habit once?

_____

_____

_____

_____

_____

Any other notes for this habit?

_____

_____

_____

_____

_____

New Habit to Make

Law 1
- What is the habit you want to make?
- When and where will it be done? (Maybe use one of Clear's patterns: "I will [BEHAVIOR] at [TIME] in [Location]" or "After [CURRENT HABIT], I will [NEW HABIT]".)
- How can you set up your environment to make it easy and obvious to do?
- How else can you make obvious cues to prompt you to do the habit?

_____
_____
_____
_____
_____

Law 2
- What's motivating you to do this habit?
- Is there some reward you will get or give yourself if you accomplish the habit? or maybe a rewarding activity right before the habit?
- Are there other people to help push you to do this habit?

_____
_____
_____
_____

Law 3
- How can you make it easier to do the habit?
- Can the environment or your schedule be set up so that the habit can be accomplished more easily?
- Can you automate or simplify your habit?
- Will Clear's "Two-minute Rule" help?

_____
_____
_____
_____
_____

Law 4
- How will this habit be more satisfying?
- Will you reward yourself for completing it?
- Will you use a habit tracker for this habit? (see page 9)
- What will you do if you fail to do the habit once?

_____

_____

_____

_____

_____

Any other notes for this habit?

_____

_____

_____

_____

_____

New Habit to Make

Law 1

- What is the habit you want to make?
- When and where will it be done? (Maybe use one of Clear's patterns: "I will [BEHAVIOR] at [TIME] in [Location]" or "After [CURRENT HABIT], I will [NEW HABIT]".)
- How can you set up your environment to make it easy and obvious to do?
- How else can you make obvious cues to prompt you to do the habit?

_____

_____

_____

_____

_____

Law 2

- What's motivating you to do this habit?
- Is there some reward you will get or give yourself if you accomplish the habit? or maybe a rewarding activity right before the habit?
- Are there other people to help push you to do this habit?

_____

_____

_____

_____

_____

Law 3

- How can you make it easier to do the habit?
- Can the environment or your schedule be set up so that the habit can be accomplished more easily?
- Can you automate or simplify your habit?
- Will Clear's "Two-minute Rule" help?

_____

_____

_____

_____

_____

Law 4

- How will this habit be more satisfying?
- Will you reward yourself for completing it?
- Will you use a habit tracker for this habit? (see page 9)
- What will you do if you fail to do the habit once?

_____

_____

_____

_____

_____

Any other notes for this habit?

_____

_____

_____

_____

_____

New Habit to Make

Law 1
- What is the habit you want to make?
- When and where will it be done? (Maybe use one of Clear's patterns: "I will [BEHAVIOR] at [TIME] in [Location]" or "After [CURRENT HABIT], I will [NEW HABIT]".)
- How can you set up your environment to make it easy and obvious to do?
- How else can you make obvious cues to prompt you to do the habit?

_____

_____

_____

_____

_____

Law 2
- What's motivating you to do this habit?
- Is there some reward you will get or give yourself if you accomplish the habit? or maybe a rewarding activity right before the habit?
- Are there other people to help push you to do this habit?

_____

_____

_____

_____

Law 3
- How can you make it easier to do the habit?
- Can the environment or your schedule be set up so that the habit can be accomplished more easily?
- Can you automate or simplify your habit?
- Will Clear's "Two-minute Rule" help?

_____

_____

_____

_____

Law 4

- How will this habit be more satisfying?
- Will you reward yourself for completing it?
- Will you use a habit tracker for this habit? (see page 9)
- What will you do if you fail to do the habit once?

_____

_____

_____

_____

_____

Any other notes for this habit?

_____

_____

_____

_____

_____

New Habit to Make

Law 1
- What is the habit you want to make?
- When and where will it be done? (Maybe use one of Clear's patterns: "I will [BEHAVIOR] at [TIME] in [Location]" or "After [CURRENT HABIT], I will [NEW HABIT]".)
- How can you set up your environment to make it easy and obvious to do?
- How else can you make obvious cues to prompt you to do the habit?

_____

_____

_____

_____

_____

Law 2
- What's motivating you to do this habit?
- Is there some reward you will get or give yourself if you accomplish the habit? or maybe a rewarding activity right before the habit?
- Are there other people to help push you to do this habit?

_____

_____

_____

_____

_____

Law 3
- How can you make it easier to do the habit?
- Can the environment or your schedule be set up so that the habit can be accomplished more easily?
- Can you automate or simplify your habit?
- Will Clear's "Two-minute Rule" help?

_____

_____

_____

_____

_____

Law 4

- How will this habit be more satisfying?
- Will you reward yourself for completing it?
- Will you use a habit tracker for this habit? (see page 9)
- What will you do if you fail to do the habit once?

_____

_____

_____

_____

_____

Any other notes for this habit?

_____

_____

_____

_____

_____

New Habit to Make

Law 1

- What is the habit you want to make?
- When and where will it be done? (Maybe use one of Clear's patterns: "I will [BEHAVIOR] at [TIME] in [Location]" or "After [CURRENT HABIT], I will [NEW HABIT]".)
- How can you set up your environment to make it easy and obvious to do?
- How else can you make obvious cues to prompt you to do the habit?

_____

_____

_____

_____

_____

Law 2

- What's motivating you to do this habit?
- Is there some reward you will get or give yourself if you accomplish the habit? or maybe a rewarding activity right before the habit?
- Are there other people to help push you to do this habit?

_____

_____

_____

_____

_____

Law 3

- How can you make it easier to do the habit?
- Can the environment or your schedule be set up so that the habit can be accomplished more easily?
- Can you automate or simplify your habit?
- Will Clear's "Two-minute Rule" help?

_____

_____

_____

_____

_____

Law 4

- How will this habit be more satisfying?
- Will you reward yourself for completing it?
- Will you use a habit tracker for this habit? (see page 9)
- What will you do if you fail to do the habit once?

_____

_____

_____

_____

_____

Any other notes for this habit?

_____

_____

_____

_____

_____

New Habit to Make

Law 1
- What is the habit you want to make?
- When and where will it be done? (Maybe use one of Clear's patterns: "I will [BEHAVIOR] at [TIME] in [Location]" or "After [CURRENT HABIT], I will [NEW HABIT]".)
- How can you set up your environment to make it easy and obvious to do?
- How else can you make obvious cues to prompt you to do the habit?

_____

_____

_____

_____

_____

Law 2
- What's motivating you to do this habit?
- Is there some reward you will get or give yourself if you accomplish the habit? or maybe a rewarding activity right before the habit?
- Are there other people to help push you to do this habit?

_____

_____

_____

_____

_____

Law 3
- How can you make it easier to do the habit?
- Can the environment or your schedule be set up so that the habit can be accomplished more easily?
- Can you automate or simplify your habit?
- Will Clear's "Two-minute Rule" help?

_____

_____

_____

_____

_____

Law 4

- How will this habit be more satisfying?
- Will you reward yourself for completing it?
- Will you use a habit tracker for this habit? (see page 9)
- What will you do if you fail to do the habit once?

_____

_____

_____

_____

_____

Any other notes for this habit?

_____

_____

_____

_____

_____

New Habit to Make

Law 1

- What is the habit you want to make?
- When and where will it be done? (Maybe use one of Clear's patterns: "I will [BEHAVIOR] at [TIME] in [Location]" or "After [CURRENT HABIT], I will [NEW HABIT]".)
- How can you set up your environment to make it easy and obvious to do?
- How else can you make obvious cues to prompt you to do the habit?

_____

_____

_____

_____

_____

Law 2

- What's motivating you to do this habit?
- Is there some reward you will get or give yourself if you accomplish the habit? or maybe a rewarding activity right before the habit?
- Are there other people to help push you to do this habit?

_____

_____

_____

_____

_____

Law 3

- How can you make it easier to do the habit?
- Can the environment or your schedule be set up so that the habit can be accomplished more easily?
- Can you automate or simplify your habit?
- Will Clear's "Two-minute Rule" help?

_____

_____

_____

_____

_____

Law 4

- How will this habit be more satisfying?
- Will you reward yourself for completing it?
- Will you use a habit tracker for this habit? (see page 9)
- What will you do if you fail to do the habit once?

_____

_____

_____

_____

_____

Any other notes for this habit?

_____

_____

_____

_____

_____

New Habit to Make

Law 1
- What is the habit you want to make?
- When and where will it be done? (Maybe use one of Clear's patterns: "I will [BEHAVIOR] at [TIME] in [Location]" or "After [CURRENT HABIT], I will [NEW HABIT]".)
- How can you set up your environment to make it easy and obvious to do?
- How else can you make obvious cues to prompt you to do the habit?

_____

_____

_____

_____

_____

Law 2
- What's motivating you to do this habit?
- Is there some reward you will get or give yourself if you accomplish the habit? or maybe a rewarding activity right before the habit?
- Are there other people to help push you to do this habit?

_____

_____

_____

_____

_____

Law 3
- How can you make it easier to do the habit?
- Can the environment or your schedule be set up so that the habit can be accomplished more easily?
- Can you automate or simplify your habit?
- Will Clear's "Two-minute Rule" help?

_____

_____

_____

_____

_____

Law 4

- How will this habit be more satisfying?
- Will you reward yourself for completing it?
- Will you use a habit tracker for this habit? (see page 9)
- What will you do if you fail to do the habit once?

_____

_____

_____

_____

_____

Any other notes for this habit?

_____

_____

_____

_____

_____

New Habit to Make

Law 1

- What is the habit you want to make?
- When and where will it be done? (Maybe use one of Clear's patterns: "I will [BEHAVIOR] at [TIME] in [Location]" or "After [CURRENT HABIT], I will [NEW HABIT]".)
- How can you set up your environment to make it easy and obvious to do?
- How else can you make obvious cues to prompt you to do the habit?

_____

_____

_____

_____

_____

Law 2

- What's motivating you to do this habit?
- Is there some reward you will get or give yourself if you accomplish the habit? or maybe a rewarding activity right before the habit?
- Are there other people to help push you to do this habit?

_____

_____

_____

_____

_____

Law 3

- How can you make it easier to do the habit?
- Can the environment or your schedule be set up so that the habit can be accomplished more easily?
- Can you automate or simplify your habit?
- Will Clear's "Two-minute Rule" help?

_____

_____

_____

_____

_____

Law 4

- How will this habit be more satisfying?
- Will you reward yourself for completing it?
- Will you use a habit tracker for this habit? (see page 9)
- What will you do if you fail to do the habit once?

_____

_____

_____

_____

_____

Any other notes for this habit?

_____

_____

_____

_____

_____

New Habit to Make

Law 1

- What is the habit you want to make?
- When and where will it be done? (Maybe use one of Clear's patterns: "I will [BEHAVIOR] at [TIME] in [Location]" or "After [CURRENT HABIT], I will [NEW HABIT]".)
- How can you set up your environment to make it easy and obvious to do?
- How else can you make obvious cues to prompt you to do the habit?

_____

_____

_____

_____

_____

Law 2

- What's motivating you to do this habit?
- Is there some reward you will get or give yourself if you accomplish the habit? or maybe a rewarding activity right before the habit?
- Are there other people to help push you to do this habit?

_____

_____

_____

_____

_____

Law 3

- How can you make it easier to do the habit?
- Can the environment or your schedule be set up so that the habit can be accomplished more easily?
- Can you automate or simplify your habit?
- Will Clear's "Two-minute Rule" help?

_____

_____

_____

_____

_____

Law 4

- How will this habit be more satisfying?
- Will you reward yourself for completing it?
- Will you use a habit tracker for this habit? (see page 9)
- What will you do if you fail to do the habit once?

_____

_____

_____

_____

_____

Any other notes for this habit?

_____

_____

_____

_____

_____

New Habit to Make

Law 1
- What is the habit you want to make?
- When and where will it be done? (Maybe use one of Clear's patterns: "I will [BEHAVIOR] at [TIME] in [Location]" or "After [CURRENT HABIT], I will [NEW HABIT]".)
- How can you set up your environment to make it easy and obvious to do?
- How else can you make obvious cues to prompt you to do the habit?

_____

_____

_____

_____

_____

Law 2
- What's motivating you to do this habit?
- Is there some reward you will get or give yourself if you accomplish the habit? or maybe a rewarding activity right before the habit?
- Are there other people to help push you to do this habit?

_____

_____

_____

_____

_____

Law 3
- How can you make it easier to do the habit?
- Can the environment or your schedule be set up so that the habit can be accomplished more easily?
- Can you automate or simplify your habit?
- Will Clear's "Two-minute Rule" help?

_____

_____

_____

_____

_____

Law 4

- How will this habit be more satisfying?
- Will you reward yourself for completing it?
- Will you use a habit tracker for this habit? (see page 9)
- What will you do if you fail to do the habit once?

_____

_____

_____

_____

_____

Any other notes for this habit?

_____

_____

_____

_____

_____

New Habit to Make

Law 1
- What is the habit you want to make?
- When and where will it be done? (Maybe use one of Clear's patterns: "I will [BEHAVIOR] at [TIME] in [Location]" or "After [CURRENT HABIT], I will [NEW HABIT]".)
- How can you set up your environment to make it easy and obvious to do?
- How else can you make obvious cues to prompt you to do the habit?

_____

_____

_____

_____

_____

Law 2
- What's motivating you to do this habit?
- Is there some reward you will get or give yourself if you accomplish the habit? or maybe a rewarding activity right before the habit?
- Are there other people to help push you to do this habit?

_____

_____

_____

_____

_____

Law 3
- How can you make it easier to do the habit?
- Can the environment or your schedule be set up so that the habit can be accomplished more easily?
- Can you automate or simplify your habit?
- Will Clear's "Two-minute Rule" help?

_____

_____

_____

_____

_____

Law 4

- How will this habit be more satisfying?
- Will you reward yourself for completing it?
- Will you use a habit tracker for this habit? (see page 9)
- What will you do if you fail to do the habit once?

_____

_____

_____

_____

_____

Any other notes for this habit?

_____

_____

_____

_____

_____

New Habit to Make

Law 1
- What is the habit you want to make?
- When and where will it be done? (Maybe use one of Clear's patterns: "I will [BEHAVIOR] at [TIME] in [Location]" or "After [CURRENT HABIT], I will [NEW HABIT]".)
- How can you set up your environment to make it easy and obvious to do?
- How else can you make obvious cues to prompt you to do the habit?

_____

_____

_____

_____

_____

Law 2
- What's motivating you to do this habit?
- Is there some reward you will get or give yourself if you accomplish the habit? or maybe a rewarding activity right before the habit?
- Are there other people to help push you to do this habit?

_____

_____

_____

_____

_____

Law 3
- How can you make it easier to do the habit?
- Can the environment or your schedule be set up so that the habit can be accomplished more easily?
- Can you automate or simplify your habit?
- Will Clear's "Two-minute Rule" help?

_____

_____

_____

_____

_____

Law 4

- How will this habit be more satisfying?
- Will you reward yourself for completing it?
- Will you use a habit tracker for this habit? (see page 9)
- What will you do if you fail to do the habit once?

_____

_____

_____

_____

_____

Any other notes for this habit?

_____

_____

_____

_____

_____

New Habit to Make

Law 1
- What is the habit you want to make?
- When and where will it be done? (Maybe use one of Clear's patterns: "I will [BEHAVIOR] at [TIME] in [Location]" or "After [CURRENT HABIT], I will [NEW HABIT]".)
- How can you set up your environment to make it easy and obvious to do?
- How else can you make obvious cues to prompt you to do the habit?

_____

_____

_____

_____

_____

Law 2
- What's motivating you to do this habit?
- Is there some reward you will get or give yourself if you accomplish the habit? or maybe a rewarding activity right before the habit?
- Are there other people to help push you to do this habit?

_____

_____

_____

_____

_____

Law 3
- How can you make it easier to do the habit?
- Can the environment or your schedule be set up so that the habit can be accomplished more easily?
- Can you automate or simplify your habit?
- Will Clear's "Two-minute Rule" help?

_____

_____

_____

_____

_____

Law 4

- How will this habit be more satisfying?
- Will you reward yourself for completing it?
- Will you use a habit tracker for this habit? (see page 9)
- What will you do if you fail to do the habit once?

_____

_____

_____

_____

_____

Any other notes for this habit?

_____

_____

_____

_____

_____

New Habit to Make

Law 1
- What is the habit you want to make?
- When and where will it be done? (Maybe use one of Clear's patterns: "I will [BEHAVIOR] at [TIME] in [Location]" or "After [CURRENT HABIT], I will [NEW HABIT]".)
- How can you set up your environment to make it easy and obvious to do?
- How else can you make obvious cues to prompt you to do the habit?

_____

_____

_____

_____

_____

Law 2
- What's motivating you to do this habit?
- Is there some reward you will get or give yourself if you accomplish the habit? or maybe a rewarding activity right before the habit?
- Are there other people to help push you to do this habit?

_____

_____

_____

_____

Law 3
- How can you make it easier to do the habit?
- Can the environment or your schedule be set up so that the habit can be accomplished more easily?
- Can you automate or simplify your habit?
- Will Clear's "Two-minute Rule" help?

_____

_____

_____

_____

Law 4

- How will this habit be more satisfying?
- Will you reward yourself for completing it?
- Will you use a habit tracker for this habit? (see page 9)
- What will you do if you fail to do the habit once?

_____

_____

_____

_____

_____

Any other notes for this habit?

_____

_____

_____

_____

_____

New Habit to Make

Law 1
- What is the habit you want to make?
- When and where will it be done? (Maybe use one of Clear's patterns: "I will [BEHAVIOR] at [TIME] in [Location]" or "After [CURRENT HABIT], I will [NEW HABIT]".)
- How can you set up your environment to make it easy and obvious to do?
- How else can you make obvious cues to prompt you to do the habit?

_____

_____

_____

_____

_____

Law 2
- What's motivating you to do this habit?
- Is there some reward you will get or give yourself if you accomplish the habit? or maybe a rewarding activity right before the habit?
- Are there other people to help push you to do this habit?

_____

_____

_____

_____

_____

Law 3
- How can you make it easier to do the habit?
- Can the environment or your schedule be set up so that the habit can be accomplished more easily?
- Can you automate or simplify your habit?
- Will Clear's "Two-minute Rule" help?

_____

_____

_____

_____

_____

Law 4

- How will this habit be more satisfying?
- Will you reward yourself for completing it?
- Will you use a habit tracker for this habit? (see page 9)
- What will you do if you fail to do the habit once?

_____

_____

_____

_____

_____

Any other notes for this habit?

_____

_____

_____

_____

_____

Habit to Break

Law 1
- What is the habit you want to break?
- When and where are cues that lead to this habit and how do you avoid these cues?
- How can you set up your environment to avoid cues?

_____

_____

_____

_____

_____

Law 2
- What's motivating you to get rid of this habit?
- What benefits or rewards are there is you avoid this habit?
- Are there other people to help push you to avoid this habit?

_____

_____

_____

_____

_____

Law 3
- How can you make it harder to do this habit?
- Can the environment or your schedule be set up so that the habit is difficult to do?

_____

_____

_____

_____

_____

Law 4

- How can you make it less satisfying to do this habit?
- Is there someone you can ask to watch your behavior or to whom you can be accountable to?
- Will you use a habit tracker to track not doing this habit? (see page 9)
- What will you do if you fail to break the habit once?
- Can you set up a way to make the results of this bad habit public and painful?

_____

_____

_____

_____

_____

Any other notes for breaking this habit?

_____

_____

_____

_____

_____

Habit to Break

Law 1
- What is the habit you want to break?
- When and where are cues that lead to this habit and how do you avoid these cues?
- How can you set up your environment to avoid cues?

_____

_____

_____

_____

_____

Law 2
- What's motivating you to get rid of this habit?
- What benefits or rewards are there is you avoid this habit?
- Are there other people to help push you to avoid this habit?

_____

_____

_____

_____

_____

Law 3
- How can you make it harder to do this habit?
- Can the environment or your schedule be set up so that the habit is difficult to do?

_____

_____

_____

_____

_____

Law 4

- How can you make it less satisfying to do this habit?
- Is there someone you can ask to watch your behavior or to whom you can be accountable to?
- Will you use a habit tracker to track not doing this habit? (see page 9)
- What will you do if you fail to break the habit once?
- Can you set up a way to make the results of this bad habit public and painful?

_____

_____

_____

_____

_____

Any other notes for breaking this habit?

_____

_____

_____

_____

_____

Habit to Break

Law 1
- What is the habit you want to break?
- When and where are cues that lead to this habit and how do you avoid these cues?
- How can you set up your environment to avoid cues?

_____

_____

_____

_____

_____

Law 2
- What's motivating you to get rid of this habit?
- What benefits or rewards are there is you avoid this habit?
- Are there other people to help push you to avoid this habit?

_____

_____

_____

_____

_____

Law 3
- How can you make it harder to do this habit?
- Can the environment or your schedule be set up so that the habit is difficult to do?

_____

_____

_____

_____

_____

Law 4

- How can you make it less satisfying to do this habit?
- Is there someone you can ask to watch your behavior or to whom you can be accountable to?
- Will you use a habit tracker to track not doing this habit? (see page 9)
- What will you do if you fail to break the habit once?
- Can you set up a way to make the results of this bad habit public and painful?

_____

_____

_____

_____

_____

Any other notes for breaking this habit?

_____

_____

_____

_____

_____

Habit to Break

Law 1

- What is the habit you want to break?
- When and where are cues that lead to this habit and how do you avoid these cues?
- How can you set up your environment to avoid cues?

_____

_____

_____

_____

_____

Law 2

- What's motivating you to get rid of this habit?
- What benefits or rewards are there is you avoid this habit?
- Are there other people to help push you to avoid this habit?

_____

_____

_____

_____

_____

Law 3

- How can you make it harder to do this habit?
- Can the environment or your schedule be set up so that the habit is difficult to do?

_____

_____

_____

_____

_____

Law 4

- How can you make it less satisfying to do this habit?
- Is there someone you can ask to watch your behavior or to whom you can be accountable to?
- Will you use a habit tracker to track not doing this habit? (see page 9)
- What will you do if you fail to break the habit once?
- Can you set up a way to make the results of this bad habit public and painful?

_____

_____

_____

_____

_____

Any other notes for breaking this habit?

_____

_____

_____

_____

_____

Habit to Break

Law 1
- What is the habit you want to break?
- When and where are cues that lead to this habit and how do you avoid these cues?
- How can you set up your environment to avoid cues?

_____

_____

_____

_____

_____

Law 2
- What's motivating you to get rid of this habit?
- What benefits or rewards are there is you avoid this habit?
- Are there other people to help push you to avoid this habit?

_____

_____

_____

_____

_____

Law 3
- How can you make it harder to do this habit?
- Can the environment or your schedule be set up so that the habit is difficult to do?

_____

_____

_____

_____

_____

Law 4

- How can you make it less satisfying to do this habit?
- Is there someone you can ask to watch your behavior or to whom you can be accountable to?
- Will you use a habit tracker to track not doing this habit? (see page 9)
- What will you do if you fail to break the habit once?
- Can you set up a way to make the results of this bad habit public and painful?

_____

_____

_____

_____

_____

Any other notes for breaking this habit?

_____

_____

_____

_____

_____

Habit to Break

Law 1
- What is the habit you want to break?
- When and where are cues that lead to this habit and how do you avoid these cues?
- How can you set up your environment to avoid cues?

_____

_____

_____

_____

_____

Law 2
- What's motivating you to get rid of this habit?
- What benefits or rewards are there is you avoid this habit?
- Are there other people to help push you to avoid this habit?

_____

_____

_____

_____

_____

Law 3
- How can you make it harder to do this habit?
- Can the environment or your schedule be set up so that the habit is difficult to do?

_____

_____

_____

_____

_____

Law 4
- How can you make it less satisfying to do this habit?
- Is there someone you can ask to watch your behavior or to whom you can be accountable to?
- Will you use a habit tracker to track not doing this habit? (see page 9)
- What will you do if you fail to break the habit once?
- Can you set up a way to make the results of this bad habit public and painful?

_____

_____

_____

_____

_____

Any other notes for breaking this habit?

_____

_____

_____

_____

_____

Habit to Break

Law 1
- What is the habit you want to break?
- When and where are cues that lead to this habit and how do you avoid these cues?
- How can you set up your environment to avoid cues?

_____

_____

_____

_____

_____

Law 2
- What's motivating you to get rid of this habit?
- What benefits or rewards are there is you avoid this habit?
- Are there other people to help push you to avoid this habit?

_____

_____

_____

_____

_____

Law 3
- How can you make it harder to do this habit?
- Can the environment or your schedule be set up so that the habit is difficult to do?

_____

_____

_____

_____

_____

Law 4

- How can you make it less satisfying to do this habit?
- Is there someone you can ask to watch your behavior or to whom you can be accountable to?
- Will you use a habit tracker to track not doing this habit? (see page 9)
- What will you do if you fail to break the habit once?
- Can you set up a way to make the results of this bad habit public and painful?

_____

_____

_____

_____

_____

Any other notes for breaking this habit?

_____

_____

_____

_____

_____

Habit to Break

Law 1
- What is the habit you want to break?
- When and where are cues that lead to this habit and how do you avoid these cues?
- How can you set up your environment to avoid cues?

_____

_____

_____

_____

_____

Law 2
- What's motivating you to get rid of this habit?
- What benefits or rewards are there is you avoid this habit?
- Are there other people to help push you to avoid this habit?

_____

_____

_____

_____

_____

Law 3
- How can you make it harder to do this habit?
- Can the environment or your schedule be set up so that the habit is difficult to do?

_____

_____

_____

_____

_____

Law 4

- How can you make it less satisfying to do this habit?
- Is there someone you can ask to watch your behavior or to whom you can be accountable to?
- Will you use a habit tracker to track not doing this habit? (see page 9)
- What will you do if you fail to break the habit once?
- Can you set up a way to make the results of this bad habit public and painful?

_____

_____

_____

_____

_____

Any other notes for breaking this habit?

_____

_____

_____

_____

_____

Habit to Break

Law 1
- What is the habit you want to break?
- When and where are cues that lead to this habit and how do you avoid these cues?
- How can you set up your environment to avoid cues?

_____

_____

_____

_____

_____

Law 2
- What's motivating you to get rid of this habit?
- What benefits or rewards are there is you avoid this habit?
- Are there other people to help push you to avoid this habit?

_____

_____

_____

_____

_____

Law 3
- How can you make it harder to do this habit?
- Can the environment or your schedule be set up so that the habit is difficult to do?

_____

_____

_____

_____

_____

Law 4

- How can you make it less satisfying to do this habit?
- Is there someone you can ask to watch your behavior or to whom you can be accountable to?
- Will you use a habit tracker to track not doing this habit? (see page 9)
- What will you do if you fail to break the habit once?
- Can you set up a way to make the results of this bad habit public and painful?

_____

_____

_____

_____

_____

Any other notes for breaking this habit?

_____

_____

_____

_____

_____

Habit to Break

Law 1
- What is the habit you want to break?
- When and where are cues that lead to this habit and how do you avoid these cues?
- How can you set up your environment to avoid cues?

_____

_____

_____

_____

_____

Law 2
- What's motivating you to get rid of this habit?
- What benefits or rewards are there is you avoid this habit?
- Are there other people to help push you to avoid this habit?

_____

_____

_____

_____

_____

Law 3
- How can you make it harder to do this habit?
- Can the environment or your schedule be set up so that the habit is difficult to do?

_____

_____

_____

_____

_____

Law 4

- How can you make it less satisfying to do this habit?
- Is there someone you can ask to watch your behavior or to whom you can be accountable to?
- Will you use a habit tracker to track not doing this habit? (see page 9)
- What will you do if you fail to break the habit once?
- Can you set up a way to make the results of this bad habit public and painful?

_____

_____

_____

_____

_____

Any other notes for breaking this habit?

_____

_____

_____

_____

_____

Habit to Break

Law 1
- What is the habit you want to break?
- When and where are cues that lead to this habit and how do you avoid these cues?
- How can you set up your environment to avoid cues?

_____

_____

_____

_____

_____

Law 2
- What's motivating you to get rid of this habit?
- What benefits or rewards are there is you avoid this habit?
- Are there other people to help push you to avoid this habit?

_____

_____

_____

_____

_____

Law 3
- How can you make it harder to do this habit?
- Can the environment or your schedule be set up so that the habit is difficult to do?

_____

_____

_____

_____

_____

Law 4

- How can you make it less satisfying to do this habit?
- Is there someone you can ask to watch your behavior or to whom you can be accountable to?
- Will you use a habit tracker to track not doing this habit? (see page 9)
- What will you do if you fail to break the habit once?
- Can you set up a way to make the results of this bad habit public and painful?

_____

_____

_____

_____

_____

Any other notes for breaking this habit?

_____

_____

_____

_____

_____

Habit to Break

Law 1
- What is the habit you want to break?
- When and where are cues that lead to this habit and how do you avoid these cues?
- How can you set up your environment to avoid cues?

_____

_____

_____

_____

_____

Law 2
- What's motivating you to get rid of this habit?
- What benefits or rewards are there is you avoid this habit?
- Are there other people to help push you to avoid this habit?

_____

_____

_____

_____

_____

Law 3
- How can you make it harder to do this habit?
- Can the environment or your schedule be set up so that the habit is difficult to do?

_____

_____

_____

_____

_____

Law 4

- How can you make it less satisfying to do this habit?
- Is there someone you can ask to watch your behavior or to whom you can be accountable to?
- Will you use a habit tracker to track not doing this habit? (see page 9)
- What will you do if you fail to break the habit once?
- Can you set up a way to make the results of this bad habit public and painful?

_____

_____

_____

_____

_____

Any other notes for breaking this habit?

_____

_____

_____

_____

_____

Habit to Break

Law 1
- What is the habit you want to break?
- When and where are cues that lead to this habit and how do you avoid these cues?
- How can you set up your environment to avoid cues?

_____

_____

_____

_____

_____

Law 2
- What's motivating you to get rid of this habit?
- What benefits or rewards are there is you avoid this habit?
- Are there other people to help push you to avoid this habit?

_____

_____

_____

_____

_____

Law 3
- How can you make it harder to do this habit?
- Can the environment or your schedule be set up so that the habit is difficult to do?

_____

_____

_____

_____

_____

Law 4

- How can you make it less satisfying to do this habit?
- Is there someone you can ask to watch your behavior or to whom you can be accountable to?
- Will you use a habit tracker to track not doing this habit? (see page 9)
- What will you do if you fail to break the habit once?
- Can you set up a way to make the results of this bad habit public and painful?

_____

_____

_____

_____

_____

Any other notes for breaking this habit?

_____

_____

_____

_____

_____

Habit to Break

Law 1
- What is the habit you want to break?
- When and where are cues that lead to this habit and how do you avoid these cues?
- How can you set up your environment to avoid cues?

_____

_____

_____

_____

_____

Law 2
- What's motivating you to get rid of this habit?
- What benefits or rewards are there is you avoid this habit?
- Are there other people to help push you to avoid this habit?

_____

_____

_____

_____

_____

Law 3
- How can you make it harder to do this habit?
- Can the environment or your schedule be set up so that the habit is difficult to do?

_____

_____

_____

_____

_____

Law 4
- How can you make it less satisfying to do this habit?
- Is there someone you can ask to watch your behavior or to whom you can be accountable to?
- Will you use a habit tracker to track not doing this habit? (see page 9)
- What will you do if you fail to break the habit once?
- Can you set up a way to make the results of this bad habit public and painful?

_____

_____

_____

_____

_____

Any other notes for breaking this habit?

_____

_____

_____

_____

_____

Habit to Break

Law 1
- What is the habit you want to break?
- When and where are cues that lead to this habit and how do you avoid these cues?
- How can you set up your environment to avoid cues?

_____

_____

_____

_____

_____

Law 2
- What's motivating you to get rid of this habit?
- What benefits or rewards are there is you avoid this habit?
- Are there other people to help push you to avoid this habit?

_____

_____

_____

_____

_____

Law 3
- How can you make it harder to do this habit?
- Can the environment or your schedule be set up so that the habit is difficult to do?

_____

_____

_____

_____

_____

Law 4

- How can you make it less satisfying to do this habit?
- Is there someone you can ask to watch your behavior or to whom you can be accountable to?
- Will you use a habit tracker to track not doing this habit? (see page 9)
- What will you do if you fail to break the habit once?
- Can you set up a way to make the results of this bad habit public and painful?

_____

_____

_____

_____

_____

Any other notes for breaking this habit?

_____

_____

_____

_____

_____

Habit to Break

Law 1
- What is the habit you want to break?
- When and where are cues that lead to this habit and how do you avoid these cues?
- How can you set up your environment to avoid cues?

_____

_____

_____

_____

_____

Law 2
- What's motivating you to get rid of this habit?
- What benefits or rewards are there is you avoid this habit?
- Are there other people to help push you to avoid this habit?

_____

_____

_____

_____

_____

Law 3
- How can you make it harder to do this habit?
- Can the environment or your schedule be set up so that the habit is difficult to do?

_____

_____

_____

_____

_____

Law 4
- How can you make it less satisfying to do this habit?
- Is there someone you can ask to watch your behavior or to whom you can be accountable to?
- Will you use a habit tracker to track not doing this habit? (see page 9)
- What will you do if you fail to break the habit once?
- Can you set up a way to make the results of this bad habit public and painful?

_____

_____

_____

_____

_____

Any other notes for breaking this habit?

_____

_____

_____

_____

_____

Habit to Break

Law 1
- What is the habit you want to break?
- When and where are cues that lead to this habit and how do you avoid these cues?
- How can you set up your environment to avoid cues?

_____

_____

_____

_____

_____

Law 2
- What's motivating you to get rid of this habit?
- What benefits or rewards are there is you avoid this habit?
- Are there other people to help push you to avoid this habit?

_____

_____

_____

_____

_____

Law 3
- How can you make it harder to do this habit?
- Can the environment or your schedule be set up so that the habit is difficult to do?

_____

_____

_____

_____

_____

Law 4

- How can you make it less satisfying to do this habit?
- Is there someone you can ask to watch your behavior or to whom you can be accountable to?
- Will you use a habit tracker to track not doing this habit? (see page 9)
- What will you do if you fail to break the habit once?
- Can you set up a way to make the results of this bad habit public and painful?

_____

_____

_____

_____

Any other notes for breaking this habit?

_____

_____

_____

_____

_____

Habit to Break

Law 1
- What is the habit you want to break?
- When and where are cues that lead to this habit and how do you avoid these cues?
- How can you set up your environment to avoid cues?

_____

_____

_____

_____

_____

Law 2
- What's motivating you to get rid of this habit?
- What benefits or rewards are there is you avoid this habit?
- Are there other people to help push you to avoid this habit?

_____

_____

_____

_____

_____

Law 3
- How can you make it harder to do this habit?
- Can the environment or your schedule be set up so that the habit is difficult to do?

_____

_____

_____

_____

_____

Law 4

- How can you make it less satisfying to do this habit?
- Is there someone you can ask to watch your behavior or to whom you can be accountable to?
- Will you use a habit tracker to track not doing this habit? (see page 9)
- What will you do if you fail to break the habit once?
- Can you set up a way to make the results of this bad habit public and painful?

_____

_____

_____

_____

_____

Any other notes for breaking this habit?

_____

_____

_____

_____

_____

Habit to Break

Law 1

- What is the habit you want to break?
- When and where are cues that lead to this habit and how do you avoid these cues?
- How can you set up your environment to avoid cues?

_____

_____

_____

_____

_____

Law 2

- What's motivating you to get rid of this habit?
- What benefits or rewards are there is you avoid this habit?
- Are there other people to help push you to avoid this habit?

_____

_____

_____

_____

_____

Law 3

- How can you make it harder to do this habit?
- Can the environment or your schedule be set up so that the habit is difficult to do?

_____

_____

_____

_____

_____

Law 4

- How can you make it less satisfying to do this habit?
- Is there someone you can ask to watch your behavior or to whom you can be accountable to?
- Will you use a habit tracker to track not doing this habit? (see page 9)
- What will you do if you fail to break the habit once?
- Can you set up a way to make the results of this bad habit public and painful?

_____

_____

_____

_____

_____

Any other notes for breaking this habit?

_____

_____

_____

_____

_____

Habit to Break

Law 1
- What is the habit you want to break?
- When and where are cues that lead to this habit and how do you avoid these cues?
- How can you set up your environment to avoid cues?

_____

_____

_____

_____

_____

Law 2
- What's motivating you to get rid of this habit?
- What benefits or rewards are there is you avoid this habit?
- Are there other people to help push you to avoid this habit?

_____

_____

_____

_____

_____

Law 3
- How can you make it harder to do this habit?
- Can the environment or your schedule be set up so that the habit is difficult to do?

_____

_____

_____

_____

_____

Law 4

- How can you make it less satisfying to do this habit?
- Is there someone you can ask to watch your behavior or to whom you can be accountable to?
- Will you use a habit tracker to track not doing this habit? (see page 9)
- What will you do if you fail to break the habit once?
- Can you set up a way to make the results of this bad habit public and painful?

_____

_____

_____

_____

_____

Any other notes for breaking this habit?

_____

_____

_____

_____

_____

Habit to Break

Law 1
- What is the habit you want to break?
- When and where are cues that lead to this habit and how do you avoid these cues?
- How can you set up your environment to avoid cues?

_____

_____

_____

_____

_____

Law 2
- What's motivating you to get rid of this habit?
- What benefits or rewards are there is you avoid this habit?
- Are there other people to help push you to avoid this habit?

_____

_____

_____

_____

_____

Law 3
- How can you make it harder to do this habit?
- Can the environment or your schedule be set up so that the habit is difficult to do?

_____

_____

_____

_____

_____

Law 4

- How can you make it less satisfying to do this habit?
- Is there someone you can ask to watch your behavior or to whom you can be accountable to?
- Will you use a habit tracker to track not doing this habit? (see page 9)
- What will you do if you fail to break the habit once?
- Can you set up a way to make the results of this bad habit public and painful?

_____

_____

_____

_____

Any other notes for breaking this habit?

_____

_____

_____

_____

_____

Habit to Break

Law 1
- What is the habit you want to break?
- When and where are cues that lead to this habit and how do you avoid these cues?
- How can you set up your environment to avoid cues?

_____

_____

_____

_____

_____

Law 2
- What's motivating you to get rid of this habit?
- What benefits or rewards are there is you avoid this habit?
- Are there other people to help push you to avoid this habit?

_____

_____

_____

_____

_____

Law 3
- How can you make it harder to do this habit?
- Can the environment or your schedule be set up so that the habit is difficult to do?

_____

_____

_____

_____

_____

Law 4

- How can you make it less satisfying to do this habit?
- Is there someone you can ask to watch your behavior or to whom you can be accountable to?
- Will you use a habit tracker to track not doing this habit? (see page 9)
- What will you do if you fail to break the habit once?
- Can you set up a way to make the results of this bad habit public and painful?

_____

_____

_____

_____

_____

Any other notes for breaking this habit?

_____

_____

_____

_____

_____

Habit to Break

Law 1

- What is the habit you want to break?
- When and where are cues that lead to this habit and how do you avoid these cues?
- How can you set up your environment to avoid cues?

_____

_____

_____

_____

_____

Law 2

- What's motivating you to get rid of this habit?
- What benefits or rewards are there is you avoid this habit?
- Are there other people to help push you to avoid this habit?

_____

_____

_____

_____

_____

Law 3

- How can you make it harder to do this habit?
- Can the environment or your schedule be set up so that the habit is difficult to do?

_____

_____

_____

_____

_____

Law 4
- How can you make it less satisfying to do this habit?
- Is there someone you can ask to watch your behavior or to whom you can be accountable to?
- Will you use a habit tracker to track not doing this habit? (see page 9)
- What will you do if you fail to break the habit once?
- Can you set up a way to make the results of this bad habit public and painful?

_____

_____

_____

_____

_____

Any other notes for breaking this habit?

_____

_____

_____

_____

_____

Habit to Break

Law 1
- What is the habit you want to break?
- When and where are cues that lead to this habit and how do you avoid these cues?
- How can you set up your environment to avoid cues?

_____

_____

_____

_____

_____

Law 2
- What's motivating you to get rid of this habit?
- What benefits or rewards are there is you avoid this habit?
- Are there other people to help push you to avoid this habit?

_____

_____

_____

_____

_____

Law 3
- How can you make it harder to do this habit?
- Can the environment or your schedule be set up so that the habit is difficult to do?

_____

_____

_____

_____

_____

Law 4

- How can you make it less satisfying to do this habit?
- Is there someone you can ask to watch your behavior or to whom you can be accountable to?
- Will you use a habit tracker to track not doing this habit? (see page 9)
- What will you do if you fail to break the habit once?
- Can you set up a way to make the results of this bad habit public and painful?

_____

_____

_____

_____

_____

Any other notes for breaking this habit?

_____

_____

_____

_____

_____

Habit to Break

Law 1
- What is the habit you want to break?
- When and where are cues that lead to this habit and how do you avoid these cues?
- How can you set up your environment to avoid cues?

_____

_____

_____

_____

_____

Law 2
- What's motivating you to get rid of this habit?
- What benefits or rewards are there is you avoid this habit?
- Are there other people to help push you to avoid this habit?

_____

_____

_____

_____

_____

Law 3
- How can you make it harder to do this habit?
- Can the environment or your schedule be set up so that the habit is difficult to do?

_____

_____

_____

_____

_____

Law 4

- How can you make it less satisfying to do this habit?
- Is there someone you can ask to watch your behavior or to whom you can be accountable to?
- Will you use a habit tracker to track not doing this habit? (see page 9)
- What will you do if you fail to break the habit once?
- Can you set up a way to make the results of this bad habit public and painful?

_____

_____

_____

_____

_____

Any other notes for breaking this habit?

_____

_____

_____

_____

_____

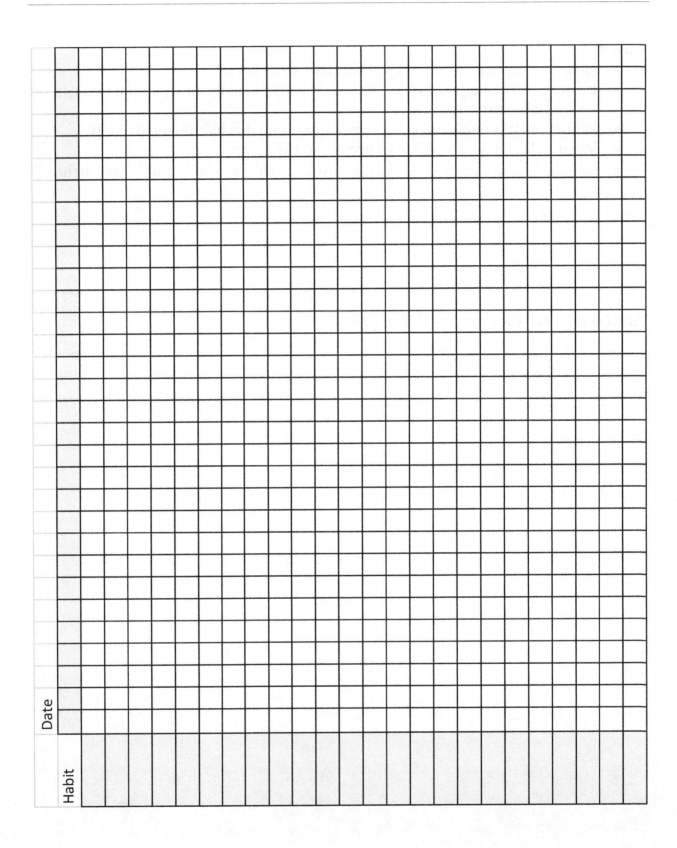

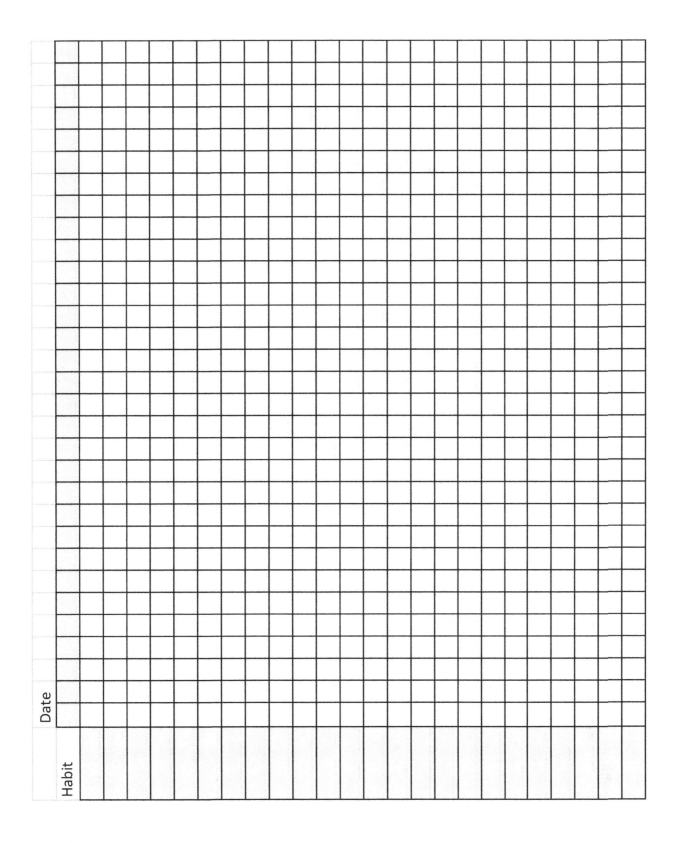

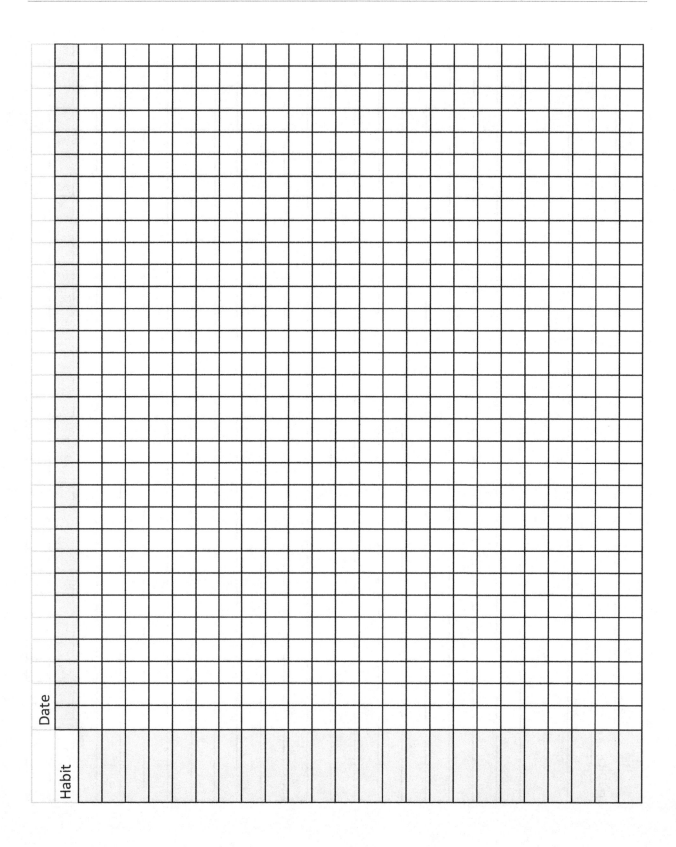

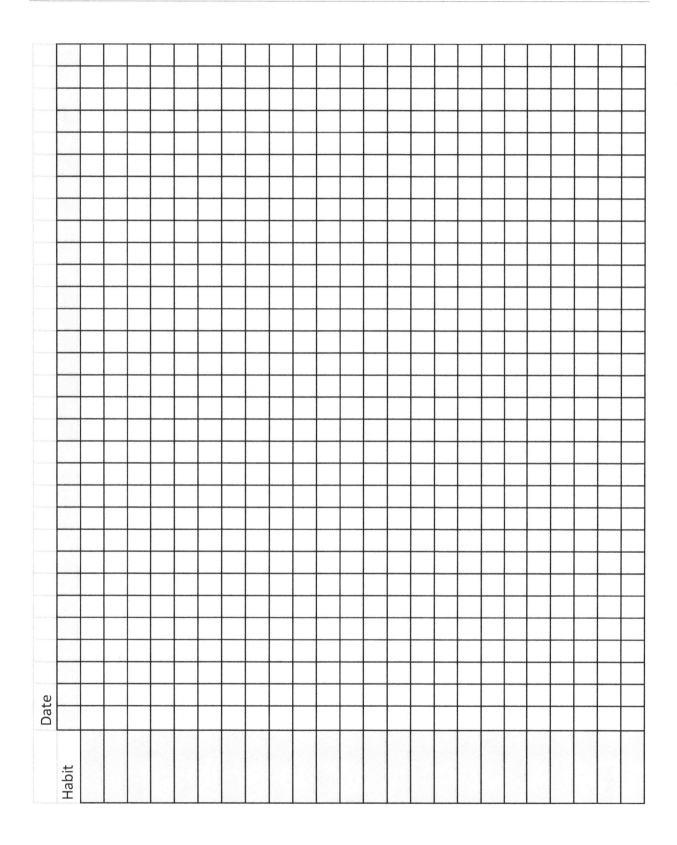

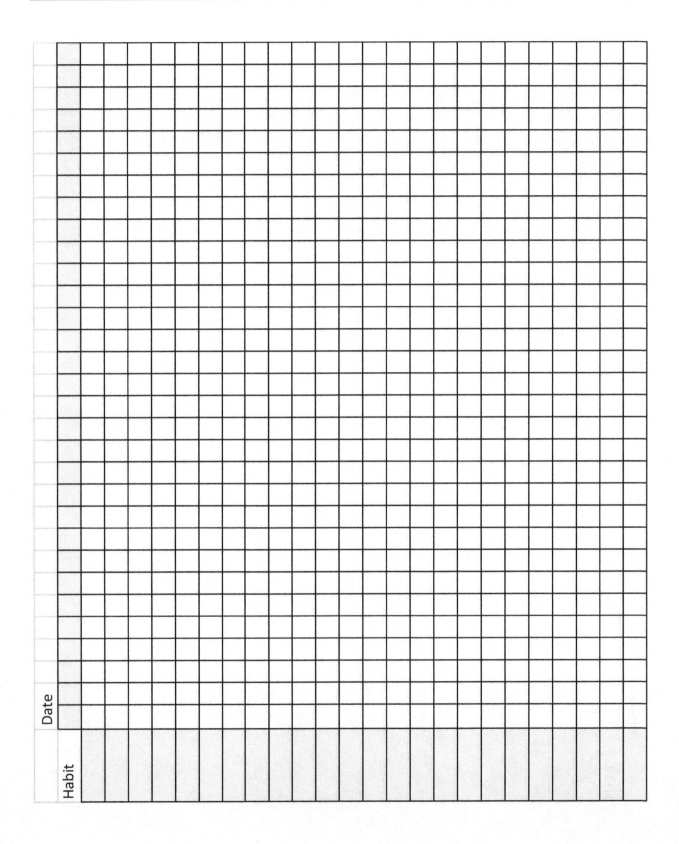

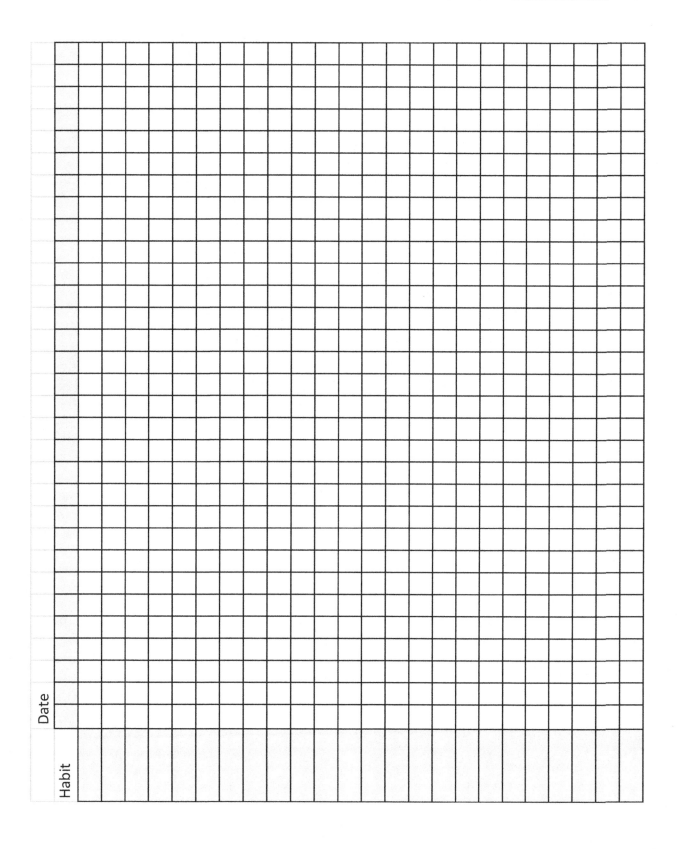

Made in the USA
Monee, IL
22 May 2024

58804122R00070